Kawhi Leonard: The Inspiring Story of One of Basketball's Best All-Around Players

An Unauthorized Biography

By: Clayton Geoffreys

Table of Contents

Foreword

Kawhi Leonard has ushered in the next era of San Antonio Spurs basketball. As Tim Duncan, Tony Parker, and Manu Ginobili near the end of their respective careers, Kawhi Leonard has emerged as the next superstar to serve as the face of the Spurs franchise. The third-youngest player to ever win the NBA Finals MVP award in 2014, Leonard has impressed players and coaches around the league for his ability to play exceptionally well on both sides of the court, making him one of the best two-way players in the game today. Kawhi's 2015-2016 All-Star selection is just the first of many to come for young Leonard, as he continues to mature and develop into the player the Spurs organization envision him becoming. Thank you for purchasing *Kawhi Leonard: The Inspiring Story of One of Basketball's Best All-Around Players*. In this unauthorized biography, we will learn Kawhi Leonard's incredible life story and impact on the game of basketball. Hope you enjoy and if you do, please do not forget to leave a review!

Also, check out my website at claytongeoffreys.com to join my exclusive list where I let you know about my latest books. To thank you for your purchase, you can go to my site to download a free copy of *33 Life Lessons: Success Principles, Career Advice & Habits of Successful People*. In the book, you'll learn from some of the greatest thought leaders of different industries on what it takes to become successful and how to live a great life.

Cheers,

Clayton Geoffreys

Visit me at www.claytongeoffreys.com

Introduction

Kawhi Leonard, as silent and discreet as he is off the NBA floor, is thought of as one of the most enigmatic and unemotional players in the whole league. But make no mistake about it because his play on the court is anything but silent and discreet. While he rarely expresses himself, Leonard's game does all the talking, and that's all we need to know. Kawhi Leonard is one of the premier two-way wing players in the whole NBA because he plays as hard on offense as he does on defense. Offensively, Leonard grew from a raw NBA prospect that was very limited regarding scoring abilities to the San Antonio Spurs' best scorer from any part of the floor. He was basically a non-threat from the perimeter, but then developed into one of the most efficient three-point shooters in the NBA. Defensively, that's where Leonard gets his meal ticket.

Coming into the NBA, the Spurs already knew that Kawhi was a defensive gem. He was always a hustle and defense guy in college. He grabbed rebounds, defended the other team's best player, and went for the 50-50 balls. Leonard translated the same game he had in college to the NBA floor, and arguably nobody else in the NBA plays perimeter defense better than he does. With a wingspan so long that his arms could envelop six men and with hands so huge that he could cover the ball with one hand, Leonard has used his natural physical gifts to good use on the defensive end of the floor.

While there are other defenders in the NBA with the same physical attributes that Kawhi has, nobody could claim the same feats Leonard accomplished in the 2014 NBA Finals. He dismantled the Miami Heat with his growing offensive repertoire while limiting LeBron James' offensive capabilities on the floor. LeBron has always been one of the toughest covers in the world because of his large frame and his wide offensive skills. He was always someone you'd rather double on offense because he could always bully his defenders.

Putting bigger defenders on him meant gambling on LeBron's quickness in getting to the basket. But Leonard shut him down on his own. He played to the physicality of the four-time MVP, and he matched James well with his unique combination of size, length, and athleticism. Playing both ends of the floor phenomenally in that Finals series earned Kawhi Leonard the accolade of Finals MVP for the San Antonio Spurs filled with household names such as Tim Duncan, Tony Parker, and Manu Ginobili. He outshined those three Spurs' veterans on his own.

Kawhi Leonard is also the poster boy for what it means to work your butt off night in and night out to become a great NBA player. While he was always a defensive gem, Kawhi's offense was not a bright spot when he entered the NBA. He struggled with handling the ball whenever he drove to the basket, and he could not make perimeter shots at a high clip to save his life. He was also playing behind Duncan, Parker, and Ginobili on offense and the three future Hall of Fame players were the ones carrying most of the offensive load for the San Antonio Spurs. But Leonard worked hard every year and his statistics and role on the team improved with each passing season.

One might argue that Leonard was just a beneficiary of playing on the Spurs, arguably the best franchise in recent years when it came to player development and system basketball. But, as good of a franchise that the Spurs are, nobody succeeds without extremely working hard. After toiling to make his name in the NBA, Leonard is now the one leading the Spurs pack and former All-Stars like Duncan, Parker, Ginobili, and Aldridge are now the ones looking up to him to lead the team to greatness. Unknown to a lot, his rise was also as silent as how he brings himself up. That's what Leonard is all about. No fuss. Just hard work and a solid basketball game.

Chapter 1: Childhood and Early Years

Kawhi Leonard was born on June 29, 1991 in Los Angeles, California, a hotbed for basketball talent. While he was born in Los Angeles, Kawhi grew up and was raised in Moreno Valley, California, just about an hour drive away from LA. The family, together with Kawhi's mother's two daughters from her previous marriage, moved to Moreno Valley when Kawhi was barely a year old. He was born to parents Mark Leonard and Kim Robertson. His father Mark gave Kawhi his name because he wanted his son to have a unique name that sounded Hawaiian. But, according to Kim, the name was from an African prince and she was the one who chose the spelling. Kawhi's parents were from your usual modern-day working class as his father owned and operated a car wash.

Mark Leonard was Kawhi's role model and idol while growing up as a child. He was the man who Kawhi always looked up to. Other than giving him that unique name, Mark taught Kawhi everything the younger Leonard knew about basketball. Kawhi got his shooting form from practicing hard with his father. Mark kept his son in tip-top shape by having him run uphill every day when there was time for Kawhi to do so. He taught his son a valuable lesson in hard work by having him assist with the car wash business. When Kawhi did not clean the cars as well as he should have, Mark would have him do it all over again to teach the young boy the value of work ethic in everything in life. Mark was the one who instilled to Kawhi how much of a valuable thing hard work is, and it stayed with the younger Leonard up to his days in the NBA. What was best about Mark's teachings to his son was that he always wanted Kawhi to keep his grades up because education was his ticket to a better and more fulfilling life if basketball ended.

Because of this kind of relationship with his father, Kawhi and Mark were technically best friends. They would even phone each other almost every night when Kawhi was playing high school basketball. Even after Mark and Kim divorced when Kawhi was five, the relationship never changed. When he would come to his father's home in Compton during summer vacation, and he would help his family by chipping in the family business and washing cars like his old man. While basketball remained his hobby, washing cars was how he got to know his father and his family better.

But, growing up as a young boy, Kawhi Leonard was never a big nor athletic kid. He was someone you could never expect to play professionally in any sport because of his limited size and athleticism. However, he was still growing, and he soon become a gifted athlete with good size and length. His work ethic was his best attribute in becoming a future pro athlete aside from his size and physical gifts. Unfortunately for Kawhi, despite being a good a basketball player, the younger Leonard would not play organized basketball until his second year in high school.

Chapter 2: High School Career

Kawhi Leonard attended Canyon Springs High School in his first two years. The school was located near home, and it was perfect for Leonard as he was always a young man who was close to his family especially, when it came to contributing to the car wash business. However, as a freshman, Kawhi did not get to play on the Canyon Springs basketball team. As Kawhi pointed out, the coach did not want him to play for some unknown reasons. Other than that, Kawhi Leonard missed the tryouts in his freshman year because he could not get a ride to the tryouts because his mother Kim was out of town that day. Despite having a seemingly valid excuse, Leonard still wasn't given a chance to play in his freshman year in high school, no matter how good of a player he already was. In the meantime, Leonard turned to football in his freshman year.

In his sophomore year, Leonard was finally given a chance to play basketball with the team. He also grew to a size of 6'4". Because Canyon Springs was such a small school with an equally low average height on the basketball team, Leonard was forced to play as a big forward dwelling inside the paint. He played like a big man in his sophomore year in high school, though he wanted to play outside the perimeter more often. What he got from this, however, was that he became a good rebounder for his size, and he brought that same ability all the way to the NBA.

Because of his desire to improve his perimeter touch and to play outside of the paint, Kawhi Leonard decided to transfer to Martin Luther King High School in Riverside, California. He had grown to his mature height of 6'7", but he wanted to hone that part of his game because he believed it was a needed aspect if he hoped to get into the NBA. Moving to King made Leonard a much-improved shooter from the outside. He became a premier perimeter threat aside from being one of the best players on his high school team. Kawhi Leonard was shooting at about 45% from three-point territory in his third year in high school. It was all a product of hard work that saw him shuffling workout and training sessions in three gyms after school just to get better as a basketball player. But then, tragedy struck.

On January 18, 2008, the 16-year old Kawhi Leonard received the saddest news he's ever heard in his entire life. Mark Leonard, the man he looked up to his whole life and the person who he regarded as his best friend, was shot to death. Mark was closing up shop at his car wash business in Compton when a group of men in a car suddenly came by. Possibly thinking that the guys wanted their car washed, Mark entertained the men, but was instead gunned to death. Even to this day, the perpetrators have not been found, and not even the motive is known. All we know was that Kawhi Leonard lost the most important man in his life that day.

After the incident, everybody looked for Kawhi, but there was no sign of him. He was then found in his room without any emotion. When asked about his feelings, the unemotional Leonard only said he was good. Twenty-four hours after the incident, Kawhi decided to play in a game against Dominguez High School. His team would lose that game, and Kawhi scored 17 points. After that loss, Leonard was seen coming up to his mom on his knees breaking down in tears, not because of the loss, but because he was so filled with emotions that he could barely contain them. Mark was supposed to be out there watching him from the stands. Instead, Kawhi's father was up there in the afterlife looking out for his son.

Leonard was not the same player as he was before his dad's death. He lost his shooting touch from the outside, and he was often lost within himself. After all, he had lost the man who he regarded as his role model. Kawhi would not talk to anyone after that incident. He kept things to himself and his family kept him out of the media's attention. He had to get back into form away from media coverage. That was always the type of guy he is.

In the ultimate way of showing tribute to his father, Kawhi Leonard worked his butt off to get back into playing shape and to get better as a player. He did not want Mark to see him the way he was at that point. His father thought him enough about hard work for Kawhi to not give in to grief. Kawhi Leonard worked just as hard as he ever did to get better as a player to fulfill his and Mark's ultimate NBA dream. In a win against the top team in the region, Leonard scored 22 points to lead King High School in a semi-final overtime thriller. As teammates pointed out, he got his shot back, and he already had the courage to smile again. Kawhi Leonard averaged 17.3 points, 6.5 rebounds, 1.7 steals, and 1.3 blocks as a junior.

Leonard further evolved into a star in his senior year with King. He needed to do so because he had not gotten the attention of college programs in his junior year. Not getting into a good college basketball program could mean the end of his dreams of being an NBA player. With that, Kawhi and future NBA player Tony Snell were among the best duos in high school basketball that season as they led King High School to a 30-3 win-loss record.

In a game against the undefeated Mater Dei High School, Kawhi Leonard displayed his all-around prowess in defense and hustle. He would score only 11 points, but he grabbed 20 boards, blocked six shots, and stole the ball three times in leading King High School to the CIF-Southern Section Division I-AA championship. With his efforts that year, he was named California's Mr. Basketball, averaging 22.6 points, 13.1 rebounds, 3.9 assists, and three blocks. Though he was ranked 8th nationally among small forwards, there weren't a lot of colleges interested in Leonard. He was under-recruited but, luckily, San

Diego State University was interested in taking the talents of the versatile forward named Kawhi Leonard.

Chapter 3: College Career

Freshman Year

Before going to college in San Diego State, Kawhi Leonard had already claimed he would stay only two years in college. That's what he told his uncle, Dennis Robertson. Two years were all he needed to be good enough to get drafted into the NBA. But during his two years with the San Diego Aztecs, he played mostly as a power forward instead of his usual place out on the perimeter. Nevertheless, Kawhi Leonard was an instant star and started in 69 out of the 70 games that he played in his two seasons.

Playing the power forward position, Kawhi Leonard was a double-double machine, if not a high scoring threat. He was the leading rebounder in the Mountain West Conference even as a freshman, and also had the most offensive rebounds that season. Aside from that, Leonard was also showing his abilities on hustle and defense, and was also one of the best in steals in the conference. His scoring needed work, but he still made it in the top 10 of the conference as a rookie. He also had 17 double-doubles that year. That was a school record for freshmen.

In his rookie season as a college student with San Diego State, Kawhi Leonard averaged 12.7 points, 9.9 rebounds, and 1.4 assists. He was named MWC Freshman of the Year and was also the MWC Tournament MVP that season. Kawhi was the first ever freshman in MWC history to be named to the First Team All-Conference. Leonard's efforts helped the Aztecs to a 25-9 win-loss record in the MWC that year and the school was an automatic entry into the NCAA tournament. In the first round of the NCAA, Kawhi Leonard had a double-double performance in a losing effort against the University of Tennessee.

Sophomore Season

Kawhi Leonard was an even better player in his sophomore season with San Diego. Much of his improvement came from his hard work. In his free time, Leonard would go to the San Diego State gym to practice on his shots. He would even bring his own lights, especially when it got dark at night or early in the morning because he wanted the school to save some money on lights because Kawhi was the only one in the gym practicing. Though Leonard was impactful in his first year in the Mountain West Conference, he still was not good enough to get the attention of NBA teams. He was a raw prospect that relied more on his physical and athletic gifts than on his basketball skills. The extra work in the offseason would make Leonard a better player because he would polish his offensive skills, particularly in shooting to become one of the Aztecs' best scorers.

He was once again the leading rebounder of the conference as well as the leading offensive rebounder. Kawhi was a far different player from his high school days where he would mostly dwell outside of the paint to shoot jump shots. In his career with the Aztecs,

Leonard was a rebounder, an energy guy, a hustle player, and a defender (fourth in steals in the MWC). Though he was fourth in scoring in the MWC that season, offense was not his forte. Kawhi would only score whenever he needed to do so.

In the whole nation, Kawhi Leonard was still a standout guy as he was 9th overall in rebounding and was fourth in total double-doubles that season with 23. He was simply a do-it-all machine in college as a power forward who was tasked to rebound night in and night out for his team though that part of his game was not his specialty. Rebounding became Leonard's calling card in his sophomore season. He had 23 games of more than ten rebounds and those included five games of more than 15 rebounds. His best rebounding game was against UNLV wherein he pulled down 17 boards to go along with 14 points for a double-double performance.

Though scoring was not the best facet of his game in college, Kawhi Leonard led San Diego in scoring 16 times that season. He had 33 games of double-figure scoring, and his best scoring game was against San Francisco wherein he scored 23 points and had 14 rebounds for one of his 23 double-double performances. In his sophomore season, Kawhi averaged 15.5 points, 10.6 rebounds, 2.5 assists, and 1.4 steals. He shot 44.4% from the floor and about 76% from the free throw line. He was once again First Team All-Conference and First Team All-Defense in the MWC. Aside from garnering a lot of accolades in the MWC, Leonard was also one of the most heralded men in the whole nation. He was named Second Team All-American by the Associated Press and Third Team All-American by the State Farm Coaches. Kawhi was also one of the candidates for both the John Wooden and Naismith awards that year.

With Kawhi Leonard leading the team in almost every facet of the game, the San Diego State Aztecs improved to a record of 34-3. They won the MWC Championships for the second straight season and were once again a shoe-in for the NCAA tournament. San Diego and Leonard would make it past the first round and into the Sweet 16. However, they lost to the eventual tournament winners, the University of Connecticut Huskies led by Kemba Walker.

In his two years at San Diego State, Kawhi Leonard had a total of 40 double-doubles, which ties 7-foot center Andrew Bogut for the most double-doubles in MWC history. He also has the second-most double-doubles in school history behind the 61 of Michael Cage. In two seasons, Leonard averaged a total of 14.1 points, 10.2 rebounds, 2.2 assists, and 1.4 steals. However, his game in college was in stark contrast to his high school self. Back in Riverside, Kawhi was an outside threat who, at one point, was a 45% shooter from three-point territory. But in college, Leonard's outside shooting numbers were awful as he converted only 25% of his attempts from beyond the arc. But

Leonard was set on fulfilling his NBA dreams as he declared to his uncle two years prior that he would only spend two seasons in college.

Even with all his accolades in college, Kawhi Leonard was still unheralded and unnoticed as a possible lottery prospect or even a potential game-changing draftee in the 2011 NBA Draft. Leonard had not proven himself as a good scorer in college and was an undersized player at his playing position with San Diego State. He was also playing in an uncompetitive conference in the NCAA. Other than that, the NBA at that time put more premium on point guards than on wing players as the league was transitioning into an era of reliance on point guards. And even outside of the point guards, guys like Tristan Thompson and Bismack Biyombo, who were both also undersized for their respective positions, were garnering more attention though they were simply players that focused solely on defense. On Leonard's part, he was a good defender, a capable rebounder, and contributor on offense, but he was still struggling with finding his niche and with focus as a player.

Chapter 4: Kawhi Leonard's NBA Career

Getting Drafted

Coming into the 2011 NBA Draft, Kawhi Leonard was a sure pick in the first round of the draft. However, nobody was too keen on the 19-year old forward. There were a lot of factors that played into that. First, he was a combo forward in college who played mostly the big man's position instead of outside the perimeter. While that wasn't necessarily a bad thing, what turned teams off was that Kawhi was merely about 6'7" and was a little undersized to play the power forward position in the NBA. Second, Leonard was never a high volume scorer in college, especially when compared to other NBA prospects that year such as Kyrie Irving, Brandon Knight, and Kemba Walker. And lastly, Kawhi did not play in a particularly competitive conference, nor did he even have a successful run in the NCAA tournament.

Nevertheless, Kawhi Leonard was still a good prospect in the NBA especially because of his defensive energy and his rebounding tenacity. Leonard was seen as a hybrid forward who could be compared to guys like Luc Richard Mbah a Moute and Gerald Wallace at his best. He was compared to those players because of how they were similarly built in athleticism and size as Leonard was about 6'7" and with an NBA body of 225 lbs. While he was always an athletic guy at his size, Leonard's best assets were his length and his hands. Kawhi's wingspan was measured at about 7'3", though he was not a particularly tall forward. But his hands were simply enormous as they were measured to be more than 11 inches, almost a foot long.

The 2011 NBA Draft was a class filled with promising guards. Guards such as Kyrie Irving, Brandon Knight, Kemba Walker, Jimmer Fredette, and Klay Thompson were the talks of that draft class. Meanwhile, the wing players and forwards such as Derrick Williams, the Morris Twins, and Kawhi Leonard were a little unheralded though Williams was slated to be the second best prospect that year. Though he was not heralded as one of the best prospects that season, Leonard was slated to be drafted as probably the third wing player to be taken.

Kawhi Leonard's upside compared to his other draft mates was his physical gifts as a player. He was a unique player in the sense that he was athletic enough to keep up with quick forwards but also had enough size, strength, and length to battle with the big men inside the paint. While there have been other players with the same physical attributes, Leonard played with a lot of motor, hustle, and energy on the court, though it would seem unnoticeable because he rarely displayed a lot of emotions.

Offensively, Leonard would often score with his jump shot or by hustling his way for offensive rebounds. He played a lot of power forward in college and has a little bit of post game from that experience. Leonard could shoot a turnaround fadeaway jumper from the post using his combination of athleticism and length to get enough separation from the defender. Kawhi was a threat from the deep perimeter in high school but seemingly lost the touch in his freshman season in college. But, in just a span of a year, there were noticeable improvements in his shooting form and in his consistency in hitting perimeter shots. Leonard also seemed comfortable handling the ball given that he played the forward position. It might have been a product of his huge hands that he was able to control and take care of the ball with ease.

Though Leonard seemed to be a tweener between the small and power forward positions, that aspect of his game was also an advantage. Kawhi could bully smaller defenders with his post game, and he could even outmuscle them on his way to the basket. When matched up with bigger defenders, he could cause mismatches because of his propensity for playing out in the perimeter. Kawhi's athletic quickness allowed him to blow by slower defenders on his way to attacking the rim. His long strides allow him to travel to the basket quickly, though he may not be the fastest player out there.

When talking about defense, that's where Kawhi Leonard gets his meal tickets. Leonard was always a rebounding machine in college, though he was not as big or as tall as other players of his position. He could get those rebounds because of his quick jump, his long arms, and his natural instincts of where the ball was going. When defending out on the perimeter, Leonard could shut down players from any position because of his combination of size and quickness. His long arms make it easy for him to contest shots and, in conjunction with his natural ability to anticipate passes, allows him to get a lot of steals. If a little questionable on offense, Leonard was surely a gem ready to shine defensively in the NBA.

On the other spectrum of Leonard's game, he wasn't necessarily a guy you could count on whenever you needed a basket at crucial times because he did not have the ability to create his shots and he also did not have that one offensive move that could stand out. Though he was comfortable with handling the ball, Kawhi found it difficult to break defenses down with his dribble moves because that part of his game remained unpolished. That also contributes to his inability to create shots. His jump shot has the potential of looking solid, but he couldn't hit it with a lot of consistency back in his college days especially when shooting outside of the three-point arc. And, when attempting to score inside the paint, he also looked a little tentative considering he wasn't an excellent post player outside of his turnaround jumper. Lastly, though he had all the tools of being one of the best defenders in the NBA, his defensive mindset was still far from there as he often gambled on steals or on playing the passing lanes. With that, Kawhi Leonard was a physical specimen but remained unpolished on a lot of levels.

On draft night, guys like Kyrie Irving, Derrick Williams, Brandon Knight, Kemba Walker, and Jimmer Fredette were all top 10 draft picks as predicted by many analysts. The Morris Twins were then selected as 13 and 14 in the draft. And then there was the Indiana Pacers franchise slated to pick the 15th guy in the draft. The Pacers, at that time, were off from a bad but hopeful season as they were banking on their high-scoring forward Danny Granger and the development of their long rookie wingman Paul George. That team needed a steady point guard to run their offense, and another wingman was the guy they would choose given that their small forward rotation was already full of talented players. That was when the San Antonio Spurs came in.

The Spurs franchise was always one of the most successful teams and was one of the best organizations in the whole NBA. But ever since losing their perimeter defender Bruce Bowen to retirement a few years back, they had never been able to replicate a similar title run to that of their 2007 Championship year. The Spurs had tried wingmen like Michael Finley and Richard Jefferson to fill in the gap left by Bowen on the defensive end, but they just could not find the best fit into their system. They tried playing Ginobili and Danny Green in that spot, but they were too undersized.

Though the team had a good regular season run in the 2010-11 season, they were upset by the eighth-seeded Grizzlies in the first round of the playoffs. Most analysts criticized the Spurs' aging roster. Management knew this, and they wanted to get younger. Given that they had a good regular season record, the Spurs were slated to pick late in the first round. To get more skilled talent, they needed to trade upwards in the draft. As their Big Three of Duncan, Parker, and Ginobili were virtually untouchable, they had to look into younger and promising pieces for a possible trade. They looked at their 25-year old long-armed point guard George Hill.

Hill was never a slacker at the point guard position. He was Tony Parker's back-up at that spot but also played a lot of minutes as the second guard side-by-side with Parker. George Hill had a lot of potential especially as he was playing and developing in the Spurs' system. He had a lot of upsides in particular on the defensive end and could also play the role of scorer very well. But if the Spurs needed Kawhi Leonard drafted into their system, Hill had to go. But he wasn't going to a team that would bench him because the Pacers were in need of a good starting point guard. At that point, it was a fair deal as the Pacers drafted Leonard with the 15th pick to send him to the Spurs for George Hill. Leonard could not have developed in the Pacers especially with Paul George and Granger hogging all the minutes. Likewise for Hill because he would have been stuck playing backup behind Parker for several more years.

For the San Antonio Spurs, they were losing probably the best backup point guard in the whole NBA for a young rookie who was largely untested in the college ranks. Kawhi Leonard was set to be the Spurs' newest project. If history would teach us, the Spurs were always good at finding and developing gems in the draft. They developed Manu Ginobili, the 57th pick in 1999 NBA Draft, into one of the best sixth men in the NBA. Tony Parker, selected by the Spurs at the tail end of the 2001 Draft, also turned into one of the best point guards in the league. For the Spurs to give up a promising young player in George Hill, they probably saw more in Kawhi Leonard than what the average scout could see. He was going to be their bridge in the gap between the aging Big Three era to bright future of the Spurs organization. In a few years, we would see Leonard carrying the whole Spurs team on the wings of his long arms.

Rookie Season

The problem before Kawhi's rookie season was that the league went into a lockout shortly after the 2011 NBA Draft. The lockout prohibited teams from practicing or even training with their players. For Leonard, what this meant was that his adjustment and development within the Spurs' system would have to wait until labor disputes were over. Luckily, in the pre-draft combine, Kawhi Leonard was able to work out with San Antonio's assistant and shooting coach Chip Engelland. Engelland showed Leonard the flaws of his shooting form and how he should pattern it after Kobe Bryant, whose shooting form is one of the most fundamental and fluid in the whole NBA. Chip worked with the young forward for three days but then he asked Kawhi to work on adjusting his shooting form on his own because the lockout prohibited them to work out together.

The results were astonishing for Chip. He was worried that the lockout might make Leonard stagnant and lazy in training and honing his shooting form. But as the lockout ended, he saw a remarkable change in how Kawhi was able to shoot the ball with more fluidity. It was a testament to how receptive and hard-working Kawhi Leonard was. Most players don't take criticisms so easily, and most players would stick to what they've been doing their whole lives. But Leonard was unlike most players. He accepted the flaws in his shooting form and strived hard to make it more fundamental. Kawhi knew there was something wrong, and he went out to fix it right away. That was the type of player that the Spurs wanted.

For San Antonio's head coach Gregg Popovich, he knew that Leonard was coming into a system that was already in its prime. The Spurs were the best regular season team a year prior, and that was without the help of Kawhi. A lot of pressure was on the shoulders of the young forward because he was expected to deliver right away for a championship contender team especially with how he replaced George Hill, a key cog in the Spurs' system in recent years. But Popovich made things easy for Leonard. He wanted things simple for his rookie. Kawhi was expected to do only three things: defend, hustle, and make the open three. That was Bruce Bowen's role for the Spurs back when he was playing, and Popovich wanted Leonard to be like Bowen.

But Kawhi Leonard was not a Bruce Bowen, he was better. Bowen was not athletic and was not the physical specimen that Leonard is. Bruce did not have the dribbling moves that Kawhi has and was not as big as an offensive threat. While Bowen was always one of the best defenders the NBA has seen in a while, he was not Kawhi Leonard even in his prime because the younger forward has more offensive capabilities outside of a three-point shot. What this meant for Popovich was that he wasn't merely integrating a rookie into the system to defend, but he could also actually depend on that youngster to shoulder the San

Antonio Spurs in the future if he developed the right way.

For that to come from Gregg Popovich was already immense in itself. Popovich once doubted that his All-Star Tony Parker would not make it in the NBA back when he was still vying for the draft. He never thought that Parker would become one of the best point guards in the league. For him to say that he was impressed with Kawhi Leonard's skill set in the forward's rookie season was enough to instill confidence in the youngster from San Diego State.

Though he had the trust and confidence of his coach even in his rookie season, something that guys like Tony Parker and Manu Ginobili never had as rookies, Kawhi Leonard started the season flat. In his first game, he shot 2 out of 9 from the field for just 6 points. He played only 13 minutes in that match. Even as his minutes increased, Leonard struggled in his first eight games, averaging about 5 points per game on dismal shooting percentages.

But when his minutes were suddenly increased in a game against the Oklahoma City Thunder on January 8, 2012, Leonard's production jumped. You could not blame him for his lackluster performances in his first few games because he was still adjusting to the system and his teammates. But in the game against OKC, Leonard gave the Spurs a double-double performance of 13 points and ten rebounds as he showed flashes of his self when he was still in college. He shot 6 out of 10 from the floor and also had two steals. Since that game, Leonard suddenly turned up the notches as he scored in double digits in six straight games. A game after his first double-double of the season, Kawhi scored a then career high of 19 points in a loss against the Milwaukee Bucks. He also had a then career high of 4 steals in that game. He would then score 11, 11, 12, and 12 in the next four games. He played for more than 30 minutes in all six of those games.

After that six-game stretch, Kawhi Leonard slowed down a bit due to inconsistencies with minutes and in what the team asked from him. His scoring was going through a seesaw ride of ups and downs, but his defense remained the same. Leonard consistently defended the other teams' best perimeter players night in and night out. He defended LeBron James in a blowout loss to the Miami Heat. Kawhi had to deal with Kevin Durant when the OKC Thunder came into town on February 4. He had a good defensive game that night as he limited the scoring champion to 22 points while also chipping in 15 points. Aside from trying to shut down the opponents' best players, Leonard was also consistently gathering steals every game as he became the Spurs' best ball thief.

Leonard would have his best individual performance of the season in a 40-point blowout to the Portland Trailblazers on February 21. He established a new career high of 24 points while also grabbing ten rebounds for his third double-double of his rookie season. Kawhi also had a then career high of 5 steals that game though it was in an embarrassing loss.

On March 16, the Spurs' starting small forward Richard Jefferson was dealt to the Golden State Warriors in exchange for scoring forward Stephen Jackson. What that deal meant for the Spurs and Kawhi was that the rookie was now the full-time starter for the San Antonio Spurs. With Kawhi owning the starting small forward spot, the Spurs suddenly went on an 11-game winning streak predicated on Leonard's defensive tenacity. Kawhi did not score a lot in that stretch, but his defense fueled the Spurs' offense as the team saw numerous blowout wins like a 35-point win in Cleveland and a 25-point beating versus the New Orleans Hornets. After that streak ended, the team once again went on a good streak to end the season. They had nine straight wins that included eight straight games of double-digit victories. From April 16 all the way to April 20, the San Antonio Spurs beat all four of their opponents by more than 21 points. After taking care of Cleveland by 16 points, they took revenge against the Trailblazers for their 40-point loss by beating them by 35. All of that was made possible by the terrific defense of Kawhi Leonard.

By the end of the season, Leonard averaged 7.9 points, 5.1 rebounds, and a team-high 1.3 steals over 24 minutes per game. He started 39 out of the 64 games that he played. Kawhi shot 49.3% from the floor as he displayed his scoring efficiency. What was surprising was that he shot 37.6% from three after shooting just 25% in the shorter college three-point arc. It all seemed like his work in the offseason paid off especially with how he worked hard on correcting his shooting form. A little hard work always pays off. He was also named to the All-Rookie First Team that year as he helped the Spurs to a 50-16 win-loss record for the top spot in the Western Conference.

The San Antonio Spurs were tasked to face the Utah Jazz in the first round of the playoffs. The Spurs were on a roll, and the Jazz seemed like they were not the team to beat the raging machine of San Antonio. For Leonard's part, he gave the same defensive energy he's always given the Spurs. He played only 20 minutes as San Antonio easily handled Utah in Game 1. Kawhi had 6 points and two steals in that game. In Game 2, it was an even bigger rout as the Spurs handled the Jazz with a 31-point win. Leonard scored a very efficient 17 points on 6 out of 7 shooting from the floor including three out four from beyond the arc. He had two steals that night once again.

While playing only about 15 minutes in Game 3, Kawhi Leonard scored only 2 points, but the Spurs did not even need him on the floor because it was once again an easy victory. Though Game 4 was more tightly contested, San Antonio came out with the victory and with the ticket to the second round via a four-game sweep of Utah Jazz. Kawhi had three points on a lone three-point basket that game.

After the easy first round win against the Jazz, the Spurs had a long vacation before they were matched up against the rejuvenated Los Angeles Clippers team led the high-flying power forward Blake Griffin and by the best pure point guard in the game Chris Paul. Paul was an offensive weapon for the Clippers whether by scoring or by passing. If there was a perimeter player Kawhi Leonard needed to cover, it was Paul.

In Game 1, as Leonard shuffled defensive duties between Chris Paul and scoring forward Caron Butler, the Spurs were again able to get a massive blowout victory. Chris Paul was held to merely 6 points that game as the long arms and the huge hands of Leonard shadowed him throughout the whole match. Kawhi also contributed with 16 points in that game as well as three steals. Game 2 was no different. It was all Spurs as they rolled on to a 17-point win for their sixth straight playoff win. Kawhi Leonard only had 5 points that game, but he once again limited the contributions of Chris Paul on offense. He also had two steals.

Leonard had a good stat line in Game 3. The rookie forward scored 14 points, grabbed nine rebounds, and had two steals in the ballgame as the Spurs raced on to a 3-0 lead over the Clippers in the series. Once again, Kawhi limited Paul, who shot 5 out of 17 for 12 points. Game 4 would be more contested for the Spurs, but the Clippers just did not have enough fight in them to extend the series even further. The Spurs swept their opponents once again and were headed hot and vigorous into the Western Conference Finals on an eight-game playoff winning streak.

After another long vacation, the San Antonio Spurs would find out that their next opponents were the younger and faster Oklahoma City Thunder. The Thunder banked on their trio of young stars, namely scoring champion Kevin Durant, mercurial point guard Russell Westbrook, and Sixth Man of the Year James Harden. All three of those players were perimeter oriented, and Kawhi Leonard indeed had his big hands full. But among that trio of stars, Durant was the most dangerous and Leonard needed to bring his A-game to stop the scoring machine.

In Game 1, Kawhi helped the Spurs limit Durant to 27 points on less than 50% shooting as San Antonio went to win their 9th straight game in the playoffs. Leonard chipped in 7 points and seven boards that match. In Game 2, Leonard had his best playoff game in his young career as he went on to score 18 points and grab ten rebounds for his first playoff double-double. Though the trio of Durant, Westbrook, and Harden combined for 88 points, the Spurs were able to shut down the rest of the Thunder on their way to their 10th straight win in the postseason.

After winning Game 2 of the Western Conference finals, the Spurs were looking like they were inching closer to another sweep. The last team to sweep every opponent on the way to the NBA Finals were the 2001 Los Angeles Lakers. Were the Spurs the next in line? The answer was in the negative because the Thunder regrouped in Game 3. OKC played team basketball and did not rely on the scoring prowess of their three perimeter players. There was only so much that Kawhi Leonard could do on the defensive end as he could not stop all the Thunder players from scoring. The Spurs ended up losing that game by 20 as their postseason winning streak ended. Leonard only had 2 points that game.

Leonard would bounce back on the individual level in Game 4. He had 17 points on 7 out of 8 shooting including 3 out of 4 from downtown. Kawhi also grabbed nine rebounds for a near double-double performance. However, he could not stop Kevin Durant from pouring in 36 points as the Thunder tied the series 2-2. Leonard would return to his inconsistent self in Game 5 as the Thunder took the series lead from the Spurs. Kawhi only had 4 points while his defensive assignment had 27. The rookie forward was once again unable to contain the scoring champion who had 34 points in Game 6. Kawhi tried to match the 48 minutes of Kevin Durant but just could not keep up. The rookie only had 5 points that game as the Spurs failed to stop the Thunder rally that helped them win four straight games in the Western Conference Finals to dispatch the San Antonio Spurs and to end their older opponents' dreams of returning to the NBA Finals.

With the San Antonio Spurs bowing out of the playoffs that season via a four-game run by the Oklahoma City Thunder, people began to question once again whether the Spurs still had enough gas in the tank for another title run considering that the Western Conference was full of young teams waiting to pounce on them. The Spurs were old as they kept banking on the aging stars of Tim Duncan, Manu Ginobili, and Tony Parker. That was how the Thunder beat them. Durant, Westbrook, and Harden were all decades younger than the Spurs trio, and their fresh legs helped them get the best out of San Antonio. As father time always wins, the Spurs knew that they had to rely on the development of their young Kawhi Leonard to help usher in a new Spurs era that does not rely heavily on the services of their three aging stars.

First Trip to the NBA Finals

In his second season in the NBA, Kawhi Leonard was set to be the starting small forward for the San Antonio Spurs with the 34-year old Stephen Jackson playing off the bench. Aside from that, Gregg Popovich loved Leonard's defensive tenacity and hustle on both ends of the court. On the Spurs' side of things, they did not change a single thing in their core group of players. They did not care about the critics pointing out their star players' advanced age, nor could they care any less about how the other teams in the Western Conference were improving. The LA Lakers had acquired All-Stars Dwight Howard and Steve Nash in the offseason. Meanwhile, the Houston Rockets were shaping up to be contenders because of the addition of James Harden to the lineup. The only positive thing that the Spurs could pick up from the offseason was that the OKC Thunder got a little weaker without their third star Harden. All else the same, the Spurs were still looking like one of the top teams in the NBA.

Kawhi Leonard had a good first game for the season. Matched up with the New Orleans Hornets, Leonard scored 19 points, grabbed seven rebounds, and stole the ball five times. The next night, in a rematch of the Western Conference Finals, Kawhi Leonard helped in limiting the Thunder's superstars though he would only score 6 points. He had five steals for the second straight game. Leonard would play inconsistently on the offensive end up until his ninth game of the season. In a match against the New York Knicks, Kawhi limited Carmelo Anthony to 9 points on 3 out of 12 shooting while also contributing 16 points, 9 rebounds, and two steals.

However, after that loss to the Knicks, Kawhi Leonard was sidelined by the Spurs' coaching staff. An MRI showed that the sophomore forward was suffering quadriceps tendinitis in his knee. The coaching staff decided that Leonard would have to be shut down for about 10 to 14 days due to the injury. Before Leonard's injury, the San Antonio Spurs were 7-2 in the season. He was averaging 10.6 points, 5.4 rebounds, and 2 steals in barely 29 minutes.

Unfortunately, the two-week rest turned out to be longer. The Spurs were still winning games due to their balanced way of playing basketball. To safeguard the future of their franchise, they decided to rest Leonard for a longer period to make sure that the injury wouldn't linger throughout the season. Leonard returned on December 21, 2012 after missing games until November 17. In his return game after a five-week absence, Leonard played off the bench to score 8 points on merely 20 minutes. A game later, Kawhi scored 17 points and had five steals in only 26 minutes as the Spurs blew the Dallas Mavericks out with 38 points. After his return to the lineup, the Spurs went on a 7-game run where Leonard was +14 when he was on the floor.

In the next set of games, Leonard would go off and on when it came to offensive production. There were nights where he would score in double digits, and there were games where he would only contribute around 5 to 10 points. But his defense never wavered in any of those games. From January 13 up to early February of 2013, the Spurs went on an 11-game winning streak and Kawhi played in 10 of those games. He was +9.7 in that streak. A game after the 11-game streak ended, Leonard recorded his best regular season scoring game as he scored 26 points on 11 out of 18 shooting. Because of his efforts, Leonard was chosen to play in the Rising Stars Challenge wherein he posted 20 points and seven rebounds in a victory for Team Chuck.

From February to March, Kawhi Leonard went 13 games of scoring in double digits including a 24-point, 13-rebound double-double performance in a win against the Cleveland Cavaliers on March 16. Two games later, Leonard would reach the 20-point mark again as he scored 21 against the Utah Jazz. He then scored back-to-back 20-point games on April 4 and 6. He had 24 points and 14 rebounds in a loss against the Thunder and then had 23 points in a tight win against the Atlanta Hawks.

By the end of the season, Kawhi Leonard was the Spurs' third-leading scorer behind Tony Parker and the rejuvenated Tim Duncan. In the 58 games that Leonard played, he averaged 11.6 points, six rebounds, and 1.7 steals on 31 minutes per game. His field goal and three-point percentages were more or less the same from the previous season though he was attempting more shots. His free throw clip increased to 82.5% from 77.3%. At the end of the season, the Spurs, with a 58-24 win-loss record, were the second best team in the West behind only the Oklahoma City Thunder.

Matched up against the Kobe-less Los Angeles Lakers that struggled to get into the playoffs, it seemed like the Spurs were on their way to an easy entry into the second round. In Game 1 of the series, the Spurs beat the Lakers by 12 as he recorded 11 rebounds and two steals. He then scored 16 in an 11-point victory in Game 2. Game 3 was an absolute destruction of the Lakers as the Spurs won the game by 31. Leonard needed only 27 minutes in that game as he scored 12. The Spurs easily dispatched the Lakers in four games after beating them in Game 4 by 21. Leonard had 13 in that match.

The San Antonio Spurs went on to face the young and dangerous Golden State Warriors in the second round. The Warriors relied heavily on their perimeter shooting, especially with the best three-point shooting duo of Stephen Curry and Klay Thompson leading them in the backcourt. Defensively, Leonard had to shut down one or the other for the Spurs to escape unscathed.

Game 1 of the series went on an epic double overtime. Due to a good shooting display from Stephen Curry, who had 44 that night, the Warriors were up by 14 in the final four minutes of the game. However, the Spurs' defense operated to shut their opponents down in that span of time as the Warriors only made 1 of their nine shots. Danny Green hit a three-point shot that sent the game into overtime. The Spurs' Ginobili narrowly missed an attempt to win the game in the first overtime, and the game went into double OT. The grit and experience of the Spurs won out in the second overtime as they escaped with a one-basket victory. Leonard had an excellent game with 18 points.

Kawhi Leonard would have a double-double performance in Game 2 as he scored 11 points and grabbed 12 rebounds. He also had two blocks and a steal. However, he could not contain the 34-point explosion of Klay Thompson, who led the way for the Warriors in taking Game 2 away from San Antonio. The Spurs would shut down both of the Warriors' shooters in Game 3 to win it by 10 points. Leonard had 15 points and nine boards that night. Game 3 would go into overtime once again. That time, it was the Warriors' turn to take the OT victory as their seemingly non-existent defense suddenly came out of nowhere to limit San Antonio to merely 3 points in the extra period. The Spurs bounced back in Games 5 and 6. Leonard had 17 in Game 5 and a double-double performance of 16 points and ten rebounds in the Game 6 closeout. He had two steals in each of those games as the Spurs were on their way to the Western Conference Finals for the second straight season.

Things turned out for the best for the San Antonio Spurs in the Western Conference Finals. In the first round, Russell Westbrook of the Oklahoma City Thunder suffered a season-ending injury at the hands of the Houston Rockets' Patrick Beverley. Without Westbrook, the Thunder were easily handled by the defense of the Memphis Grizzlies in the second round. Without their tormentors from a season ago, the Spurs were eyeing on a possible appearance in the NBA Finals, their first since 2007.

The Grizzlies' defense were always the most feared and vaunted in the whole NBA landscape. They shut down Kevin Durant in the second round as he was seemingly a one-man team. But the Spurs were different. They relied on a lot of ball movement to free up shooters and cutters inside the paint. The Grizzlies relied on ball pressure. But ball pressure is useless against the best ball movement in the league. Game 1 proved that as the Spurs went on to win it by 22. Leonard barely played 30 minutes that night but scored 18 points, his best yet that postseason.

Game 2 was more hotly contested as the Grizzlies managed to force overtime with their tight defense. But the Spurs still came out with the W with Leonard scoring 12. Game 3 was set in Memphis, but nothing changed, even with the different scenery. Limited to just 4 points, which ended his 11-game playoff streak of double-digit scoring, Leonard put his energy on the defensive end as he grabbed 11 rebounds to help win the game for San Antonio by 11 points. Kawhi would record five steals in Game 4 as the Spurs quickly swept the Grizzlies in four games. That was the first Conference Finals sweep in the NBA in 10 years.

After sweeping the Grizzlies, the San Antonio Spurs had a lot of rest before finding out who their opponents would be for the NBA championship. They needed every second of rest because they were going to face the Miami Heat in the Finals. The Heat, led by four-time MVP LeBron James and together with multiple-time All-Stars Dwyane Wade and Chris Bosh, were off from one of the finest regular season records in the NBA and were the defending champions of the league. As good as the rest of the Heat were, nobody posed more challenge for the Spurs' Kawhi Leonard than LeBron James. He was regarded as the best player in the league at that time and as one of the toughest, if not the toughest, players to defend due to his combination of size, athleticism, and skill. Indeed, Kawhi had his 11-inch hands full as a lot of pressure was on his second-year shoulders.

Putting all of his efforts on defense, Kawhi Leonard deferred the offensive duties to Duncan, Parker, and Ginobili who all had good games that night. Leonard recorded a double-double in his first ever Finals appearance with 10 points and ten rebounds while playing good defense on the best player of the planet. LeBron would have a terrific triple-double performance of 18 points, 18 rebounds, and ten assists. But he only shot 7 out of 16 from the field and was always shadowed by the big hands and long arms of Leonard. The Spurs came out with a slim victory of 4 points.

In Game 2, Leonard once again limited LeBron's efficiency. James scored 17 points on seven out 17 shooting. Unfortunately for the Spurs, all of the other Heat players, especially Ray Allen off the bench, came out to play. San Antonio lost by 19 big points that night as the series was tied one win apiece. Game 3 was a display of shooting magnificence for the Spurs as they destroyed the Heat. Danny Green hit seven outside shots while Gary Neal had six. Leonard wasn't too shabby either and contributed two three-pointers on his way to 14 points and 12 rebounds. He also limited James to just 15 points on 7 out of 21 shooting. The Spurs hit a total of 16 three-pointers to beat the Heat by 36.

As good as their Game 3 performance was, the Heat bounced back in Game 4. LeBron James suddenly broke out that game and poured in 33 points and 11 rebounds. His shooting from the floor was also great as he shot 15 out of 25. Leonard, who had 12, could not do anything to stop James' explosion. The Spurs lost by 16 that game as the Heat tied the series once again. Back to playing good defense in Game 5, Kawhi Leonard limited James to 8 out of 22 shooting while also chipping in 16 points, eight rebounds, and three steals as the Spurs won by 10 to get within one game from winning the NBA championship for a fifth time in franchise history.

Game 6 was an instant classic for the Miami Heat to the dismay of the San Antonio Spurs. It was a tight game all throughout until the fourth quarter. Leonard had his best playoff performance as he scored 22 points and grabbed 11 rebounds at the end of the game. Meanwhile, his counterpart in Miami had a triple-double performance to force Game 7. With less than half a minute left on the clock, the Spurs were up by five seemingly insurmountable points.

Officials were ready to bring out the Larry O'Brien Trophy and Miami fans were already exiting the building. With 20 seconds left, James hit a three-pointer to cut the lead down to two points. In one of the worst moments of his young career, Kawhi Leonard could have sealed the game and the title if he sank two free throws after being fouled. The youth and the pressure got to him as he sank only one. On the other end of the floor, LeBron missed an outside shot but Bosh tipped it right over to Ray Allen at the right corner for a game-tying three-pointer. Bosh blocked a last-second attempt at a game-winner and the game went into overtime. The Heat fought back and crawled their way to an overtime victory to save their season and their hopes for a second NBA title. Meanwhile, the Spurs were dumbfounded by the turn of events. For Leonard's part, he was an 82.5% shooter from the foul line but missed the one shot that mattered the most. Had he made that shot, the Spurs could have sealed the 2013 championship.

Probably affected by his missed free throw in Game 6, Leonard could not stop LeBron from scoring in Game 7 though he had one of his finest all-around games with 19 points and 16 rebounds. His counterpart had 37 points including five three-pointers. The Spurs just could not contain the Heat anymore as even bench player Shane Battier was clicking from the outside with six three-pointers. In the end, the Heat won the NBA championship, and the Spurs were sent home packing even after displaying one of the best postseason performances on their way to the NBA Finals. For Leonard's part, he was still young and inexperienced, and there were still plenty of opportunities to win a title. But his experience in defending LeBron James was priceless as it seriously helped him in forging a future All-Star caliber career.

Winning the NBA Championship, Finals MVP

After a trip to the NBA Finals wherein they lost to the Miami Heat in a disappointing seven-game series, many analysts began to write off the San Antonio Spurs saying that their 2013 run was their final chance at a championship, especially because the core of Duncan, Parker, and Ginobili was aging every year. As critics began to grow, so did the confidence of the Spurs coming into the season. They did not change a single thing in their roster other than signing Marco Belinelli in place of Gary Neal. Instead of moping and feeling sorry, they got back to work during the offseason to improve their attack and their movement-heavy offense.

The missed free throw still haunted Kawhi Leonard. Had he made that one single freebie, things would have turned out better for him and his team. But seeing the veterans like Timmy, Tony, and Manu doing their share of getting better in the offseason was enough to pump up Leonard to personally improve. He was in basketball's single greatest system. That system had no room for moping around and feeling sorry. There was no use crying over spilt milk and Kawhi's only chance at redemption was to help his team get back to the NBA Finals and win it all.

It seemed that all the hard work in the offseason paid off for both Kawhi Leonard and the San Antonio Spurs. In their first 15 games, the Spurs won all but two games. Kawhi was in double figure scoring in 10 of those 15 games and he also had two double-doubles while playing pesky perimeter defense by stealing the ball at a higher rate than he ever did before. In December, he would have eight straight games of double digit scoring highlighted by his 21-point, 10-rebound double-double performance in a win against the Golden State Warriors. At that point of the season, the Spurs were consistently at the top of the Western Conference standings.

From late January up until February, Kawhi would, however, miss 14 straight games due to injury. Leonard suffered a fractured metacarpal in his right finger, his shooting hand, and was forced to be sidelined for three to four weeks. In his absence, the Spurs went 8-6. That mediocre 14-game record showed how much of a factor Leonard was for the Spurs, though he wasn't scoring as much as most other star players. His main contribution was at the defensive end where he was always at his brightest.

The Spurs missed his energy at that part of the floor, and it was evident, especially when they lost three straight games in Leonard's absence.

Kawhi Leonard returned to action on February 26, 2014 in a match against Detroit wherein he showed immediate impact. Leonard scored 15 points, grabbed six rebounds, and assisted on four baskets while both stealing and blocking the ball twice. He filled in the stat sheet even after missing a month of basketball. After his return, Leonard went on an eight-game tear of scoring in double digits. His return also sparked a remarkable run for the Spurs who went on to win 19 straight games since February 26. In those 19 games, Leonard scored in double digits 17 times. He also had two double-doubles and stole the ball at least once in 15 games. The Spurs would win 3 out of 7 after that 19-game tear but it was already elementary as they had clinched the best record in the Western Conference.

In his third season in the NBA, Kawhi Leonard averaged 12.8 points, 6.2 rebounds, and a team high 1.7 steals. His field goal percentage increased to 52.2% as he was showing an increase in his efficiency and consistency when it came to shooting. Leonard helped the Spurs to a 62-20 record as the team silenced all doubters about how they were all out of gas after losing to the Miami Heat almost a year prior. Because of his efforts, Kawhi Leonard was named to the All-Defensive Second Team at the end of the 2013-14 season.

The road to the NBA Finals wasn't going to be easy for the Spurs compared to the previous season. In the first round, they met the veteran-laden Dallas Mavericks squad, a team they have had a long rivalry ever since the late 90's. The Spurs went on to win Game 1 with the help of Leonard's double-double performance of 11 points and ten rebounds. But then they went on to lose Game 2 by 21 points. In that match, Kawhi was limited to merely 6 points.

Kawhi bounced back in Game 3 as the series shifted over to Dallas. Leonard filled in the stat sheet as he had 17 points, five rebounds, 3 assists, and 5 remarkable steals while shooting 7 out of 8 from the floor. However, the Spurs lost that one by the slimmest of margins and the Mavs were ahead in the series. The Spurs would tie the series by winning Game 4 on the road and would regain the lead in Game 5 back in San Antonio.

With only one win away from securing their ticket to the second round, the Spurs were intent on dispatching the Mavericks quickly. But Dallas had other plans as Monta Ellis and Dirk Nowitzki got a tough win on their home floor to send the series into a decisive Game 7. But the Mavs seemed to have run out of gas because the Spurs ran roughshod over them in Game 7 with a 23-point victory. In the final three games of the series, Kawhi Leonard had three double-digit scoring games while also contributing almost 7 rebounds per game.

Kawhi Leonard played one of his best playoff series in the second round of the 2014 playoffs against the Portland Trailblazers. In Game 1, he scored 16 points while also having 9 rebounds and 4 steals as the Spurs handled the Blazers with a 24-point win. Leonard displayed another remarkable performance in Game 2 as he chipped in with 20 points and two steals for the Spurs' 17-point win. The Spurs would get an insurmountable 3-0 series lead after taking Game 3 away from Portland's home floor. Kawhi had 16 points and ten rebounds.

The Portland Trailblazers, however, would take one game away from the Spurs after losing in double digits in three straight games. They won Game 4 by 11 points, but it was all they had left in the tank. In Game 5, the Spurs went back to their winning ways as they quickly destroyed the Blazers with a 22-point victory. In that closeout game, Leonard had his best game of the post season yet with 22 points, seven rebounds, and five steals. In the series against the Portland

Trailblazers, Kawhi Leonard averaged 17 points, 7.6 rebounds, and 2.8 steals.

The San Antonio Spurs were on their way to the Conference Finals. But in the way of their second straight NBA Finals appearance were the Oklahoma City Thunder. Two season prior, the Thunder beat the Spurs out in the Western Conference Finals to get into the NBA championship series. In the 2014 playoffs, the Spurs were thinking of revenge. They were now better as a team as their chemistry and ball movement had improved by leaps and bounds. Kawhi Leonard was two years better, wiser, and more experienced. Moreover, the Thunder were already without James Harden for two years. Hence, the Spurs had one less problem in the OKC Thunder's lineup.

In Game 1, the Spurs displayed their much-improved ball movement as they perplexed the OKC Thunder's defense to start the series. Banking on the individual plays of the newly minted 2014 MVP Kevin Durant and Russell Westbrook, there was little that the Thunder could do to stop the balanced offensive attack of the Spurs as the game ended with San Antonio winning it by 17. Kawhi had 16 points, six rebounds, and 3 steals that game while making things difficult for Durant. Game 2 was one of the best performances the Spurs had in recent years. They took their defense-confusing ball movement to new heights as they consistently found Danny Green open for seven three-pointers. The Spurs were so good that night that Leonard needed only to play less than 16 minutes to help the Spurs win it by 35 big points.

OKC would somehow find ways to win both of their two straight games at home. They won Game 3 by 9 points and Game 4 by 13. In both games, Leonard scored only 10 points each. But even if he was scoring less than stellar, he was still playing tough defense on Kevin Durant who was finding it difficult to score efficiently from the field. The truth was that it was

Russell Westbrook who was carrying the Thunder in those two wins.

Back in San Antonio for Game 5, it was another day in the office for the Spurs who once again blew out their opponents for the third time in the Western Conference Finals that season. They won by 28 points as the Spurs once again relied on their ball movement to open up numerous three-point opportunities for the shooters. Kawhi Leonard had 14 points that night. The Spurs would close out the series in Game 6 in the closest game of the series. They needed to rely on their superior experience to win out the final minutes of the fourth quarter as they were on their way to the NBA Finals for the second straight season. Never in Spurs history has the team been in the NBA Finals for two straight years. In Game 6, Leonard had 17 points, 11 rebounds, and four assists as he was back in the championship series to redeem the missed free throw he had the last season. In the NBA Finals of 2014, the

Spurs were set to face off against, yet again, the Miami Heat, who were thinking about a three peat.

The Spurs were much better than they were when the Heat beat them in the 2013 Finals. Though they were older, they had more chemistry and their growing star Kawhi Leonard had more experience under his belt. Leonard was once again given the most unenviable task of defending the best player in the world, LeBron James. But in 2014, he was back with a vengeance and was out on making things even more difficult for the four-time NBA MVP.

Game 1 started with the San Antonio Spurs drawing first blood much like they did in 2013. The Spurs relied on their ball movement to hit open three pointers amounting to 13 at the end of the game. The Heat had made the game close in the third quarter, but the Spurs had a phenomenal fourth quarter rally to finish the game with a 15-point win. Leonard would only score 9 in that game, but he did not make things easy for

LeBron James. The Heat would come out of Game 2 with a slim victory of only two points thanks to clutch baskets by Chris Bosh. Leonard was once again limited to 9 points in that game and shot the ball badly as he went 3 out of 9 from the floor. He even allowed LeBron James to score 35 in Game 2. But that was the worst that things would get for the young small forward out of San Diego State.

Kawhi Leonard would put the whole San Antonio Spurs on his broad shoulders and in the palm of his huge hands starting Game 3 of the 2014 Finals. Leonard displayed his growing arsenal of offensive moves as he hit pull-up jumpers after jumpers and even drained three shots from beyond the arc for 29 points. This was all thanks to the pep talk and the confidence that Popovich gave to him after Game 2. Meanwhile, he wasn't even slacking off on the defensive end as he recorded two steals and two blocks while limiting LeBron to 22 points. The Spurs won that game by 19 points.

Game 4 wasn't any different, even when the Heat were on their second home stand. The Spurs drained three-pointers after three-pointers as a display of the ball movement they've been using to dominate the rest of the league during the entire season. It was a balanced effort on offense and as starters and bench players contributed to the cause. Meanwhile, the defense also played its part as the Spurs were able to limit the other Heat players to turn them into virtually a one-man show run by LeBron James. Though the game was balanced on both offense and defense for the Spurs, one man shone brightly. That one man was Kawhi Leonard. For the second straight game in the Finals, the third-year forward top scored for the team with 20 points while also contributing 14 rebounds including five off the offensive end. His defense was even better as he had three steals and also three blocks. The Finals was slowly becoming Kawhi Leonard's show as his team won Game 4 by 21.

In his third straight marvelous Finals display, Kawhi Leonard led the Spurs once again by scoring 22 points and grabbing ten rebounds while having one apiece in the steals and blocks column. He was also making life difficult for the Miami Heat that turned to LeBron James once again to bail them out. The Spurs defense, led by Leonard, was essentially shutting down every other Heat player not named LeBron. For the Spurs' part, it wasn't even a one-man show by Kawhi because Parker, Duncan, Ginobili, and Mills were contributing to the cause of winning the franchise's fifth NBA title. The Spurs hit a total of 12 three-pointers, three of which came from Leonard. The Heat were dumbfounded and didn't know what hit them. It was an altogether different Spurs team compared to the one that the Heat beat in 2013.

At the end of the night, the Spurs found themselves winning Game 5 by 17 points. Though Kawhi Leonard fouled out of the game, he already did all that he could to help the Spurs win one of the most lopsided NBA

Finals series in league history. With the win in Game 5, the San Antonio Spurs' revenge trip was over as they were now the ones hoisting up the Larry O'Brien Trophy on their home floor. Winning the NBA Finals culminated a season for the Spurs who showed to the world how the game of basketball should be played. They played it to perfection using an array of wonderful ball movement while also putting in the same effort on defense.

With the Spurs' balanced effort on offense, there were plenty of players worthy of praise at the end of the five-game series. Tony Parker played well as he consistently poured in about 17 points in the Finals. Tim Duncan played well beyond his years even after playing almost two decades in the NBA. Manu Ginobili showed the world that he still had a lot left in the tank as one of the most dangerous players off the bench. All three of the Spurs' Big Three played well. But there was one player who had a brighter star than the three players that have all contributed to the Spurs' last four championships. That man was, you guessed it, Kawhi Leonard.

Leonard averaged 17.8 points, 6.4 rebounds, 1.8 steals, and 1.4 blocks while shooting above 60% in the series. He started the Finals less than stellar after scoring only 9 points each in Games 1 and 2. But he then exploded in the next three games as he was essentially the reason for the Spurs' fabulous rout of the Heat. For his efforts, he was named the 2014 Finals MVP and was the second youngest player to win the award. The youngest player to win Finals MVP was Magic Johnson, who won it twice at ages younger than Leonard.

What made the award and the championship trophy even special was the fact that he won it on Father's Day. It had been six years since his father had been murdered and the best gift that Leonard could ever give his father, who was surely watching from up above, was being the best player in the NBA Finals.

Winning the Finals MVP was a testament to how much his father had taught him the values of hard work and perseverance and nothing short of that award could have proved his efforts were not in vain. Kawhi had finally redeemed himself in the NBA Finals and was finally able to put his name on the NBA map. After the 2014 Finals, the rest of the NBA were on notice. Kawhi Leonard was coming for more and was just getting started.

Winning the Defensive Player of the Year Award

Other than drafting a talented young kid named Kyle Anderson in the 2014 NBA Draft, the Spurs, as always, did nothing to change their core group of players. They were happy with the championships that their Big Three was able to bring to the organization, and they were even happier with how their role players were able to help them win a title in 2014. Though the Spurs were still an aging group, they had a good core of young players led by Kawhi Leonard.

Unfortunately for Kawhi, his season did not start as good as he thought he would. Leonard missed a lot of preseason games due to an infection in his right eye. He would also miss the season-opening game on their home floor though he was present for the ring ceremony. Leonard came back in the second game of the season but he started slow in his first three games. His first solid game was a double-double performance against the New Orleans Pelicans as he recorded 14 points and 14 rebounds in a slim loss. He exploded two nights later on November 10, 2014 as he scored 26 points and grabbed 10 rebounds while stealing the ball thrice. Leonard would have four more double-double performances in his first 20 games. He would have another 26-10 scoring-rebounding performance in a win versus the Philadelphia 76ers early in December.

However, Kawhi Leonard would yet again miss a bunch of games in the 2014-2015 season as he was rested with due to injury in the middle of December up to the middle of January. Leonard suffered a torn ligament in his right hand and was forced to be sidelined for a total of 17 games. In Kawhi's 17-game absence, the Spurs lost a total of 9 games including three in a four-game losing streak. That was how important Leonard had become to the San Antonio Spurs as he was already arguably the best player in a lineup full of legendary players.

When Kawhi Leonard returned to the lineup on January 16, 2015, he immediately went back to work as he had 20 points, 4 rebounds, 5 assists, and 3 steals in a 14-point win against Portland. He would score in double digits in six straight games since his return. From late February up to the middle of March, Kawhi Leonard had the finest six-game stretch in his young career. Leonard scored more than 20 points in six straight games as he was finally displaying a newfound scoring confidence in his growing offensive repertoire. He also had two 20-10 scoring-rebounding games in that stretch while also have three steals three times and five steals once. Kawhi Leonard was steadily becoming one of the best, if not the best, two-way players in the whole NBA.

Since February 25 up to their final game on April 15, Kawhi Leonard was in double-digit scoring and was steadily putting up about more than 20 points per game in 14 of his 26 straight double-digit scoring games. He also had five double-doubles, four of which were 20-10 games. At the end of the season, Kawhi Leonard was the Spurs' leading scorer with 16.5 points while also chipping in 7.2 rebounds, and 2.5 assists. He also led the whole NBA in steals as he averaged 2.3 per game in that department. All of his numbers were then career highs as he was still improving as a young player. Because of his efforts on the defensive end and because of the fallout of his defensive dominance over LeBron in the 2014 NBA Finals, Leonard was awarded the Defensive Player of the Year Award and was also named to the NBA All-Defensive First Team.

With Kawhi's leadership over the veteran-laden San Antonio Spurs squad, the team was constantly at the second spot in the Western Conference standings behind the much-improved Golden State Warriors who were experiencing a historic season. Unfortunately, the West was so broad and so competitive that it took until the final game of the season to finally settle the playoff seeding. The Spurs could have locked up the second seed with a win over the New Orleans Pelicans in their final game. However, the Pelicans defeated them and secured the final seed in the West. Meanwhile, the Spurs dropped from the second seed all the way to the 6th with a 55-27 record.

In the first round, the San Antonio Spurs met the third-seeded Los Angeles Clippers, who were playing spectacularly throughout the whole season. The Spurs ended up losing Game 1 by 15 points thanks to an explosion by Chris Paul. Kawhi top-scored for his team with 18 while also contributing four steals to the cause. Game 2 would go into overtime as the Clippers managed to fight back in the fourth quarter. However, the Spurs got out of Los Angeles with the win thanks to the 28 points of Tim Duncan and the 23 of Kawhi Leonard.

Kawhi Leonard would have an explosive Game 3 as the Spurs blew out the Clippers in San Antonio with a 27-point win. Leonard had 32 points on 13 out of 18 from the field including three makes from beyond the arc. He also had three steals in that game. The Clippers would, however, tie the series up yet again after winning Game 4 in San Antonio. Leonard had 26 points in that match. The Spurs would take a 3-2 advantage by winning Game 5 even though Leonard shot a dismal 5 out of 16 from the field.

The Spurs were one win away from going to the second round in an effort to defend their NBA title.

They had as much as a 10-point lead but the Clippers fought back to win the game and sent the series to a do-or-die Game 7. In Game 6, Leonard shot the ball poorly again as he was merely 3 out of 15. Game 7 in Los Angeles was one of the toughest played games of the postseason. There were 31 lead changes even as Chris Paul went down with a hamstring injury. Paul later returned late in the third quarter and hit a three-pointer at the end of the quarter. The Spurs played the Clips tight in the fourth quarter and neither team gave an inch of space. With the game tied at the dying seconds and with the Clippers in possession of the ball, Chris Paul drove into the lane and jumped from the off, but healthy leg in order to hit an awkward-looking shot with merely a second left on the clock. The Spurs could not convert and the Clippers went on to win the series.

With the loss, the San Antonio Spurs were sent packing without having a chance of defending their NBA title. In the series against the Clippers, Kawhi

Leonard started high with four consecutive big games but suddenly struggled in the final three games, the ones that mattered the most. He averaged 20.3 points, 7.4 rebounds, and 1.1 steals in that series while shooting his playoff-worst percentage of 47.7%. The Spurs were overtaken by the eventual champions Golden State Warriors as the new kings of the Western Conference. With the first round exit, doubters began to resurface once again. Duncan would be 39 in the next season and Ginobili 38. Critics called out for the two elder statesmen, especially Ginobili, to retire as they seemed to have almost nothing left in their tanks. But, as history has shown, you should never count the Spurs out just yet.

Enter LaMarcus Aldridge, First All-Star Season

In the offseason prior to the 2015-16 season, LaMarcus Aldridge of the Portland Trailblazers decided to opt out of his contract because he was unhappy with how the Trailblazers could not get over the hump in the playoffs. A lot of teams were vying for the services of the All-Star power forward. Such organizations included the Los Angeles Lakers, the Dallas Mavericks, and of course the San Antonio Spurs. The Spurs had a lot of space in their salary cap as their core players had taken pay cuts a few seasons ago. They had also gotten rid of the contracts of guys like Tiago Splitter and Cory Joseph in order to make room for a huge contract signing. Aldridge, a native of Texas, was torn between San Antonio and his hometown of Dallas. But he chose the Spurs in the end due to the winning culture and to the steady system that had already been established for more than a decade. Moreover, he was going to learn from Tim Duncan, the best power forward in the game.

Other than signing an All-Star like LaMarcus Aldridge to a maximum contract, the Spurs also secured the services of their most valuable player, Kawhi Leonard. Leonard signed a contract extension worth $90 million over the next five years. He was going to be the Spurs' primary star in the future, and deserved nothing short of a max contract.

As age continued to diminish, so did the other players on the San Antonio roster. They had acquired a second towering player to pair up with Tim Duncan on the frontcourt, and Gregg Popovich suddenly decided to dump their fast-paced style of shooting three-pointers on offense to go back to their roots of playing a slow-paced defensive style of basketball predicated on midrange shots on the offense. The style suited the Spurs' aging players, especially Duncan. Meanwhile, the defense-oriented pace was up to the standards of Kawhi Leonard, a defensive specialist.

The San Antonio Spurs started the 2015-16 season like a house on fire as they seemed to be unbeatable on their home floor. Kawhi started the season with a career high of 32 points in their first game in a loss against the OKC Thunder. He also had 8 rebounds and three steals in that game. Leonard would score in double digits in his first 20 games of the season and scored more than 20 in 12 of those games. In one of those games, Leonard had one of the best performances of his season. He scored 27 points while converting 7 three-pointers in a win against the Memphis Grizzlies on December 3, 2015. With Leonard leading the way, the Spurs lost only four games in their first 20.

The Spurs continued to rack up the wins throughout the whole season and were continuing to defy odds and expectations. The team has beaten opponents using their league-leading defense and their efficient offense as they have constantly been the top team in terms of point differential. They were also virtually unbeatable in San Antonio as their home wins had extended it to a 37-game streak, a stretch that spanned the late parts of the 2014-15 season. Unfortunately, the streak ended at 37 as the LA Clippers beat them on their home court on February 18, 2016. In that game, Kawhi Leonard did not play. Nevertheless, the Spurs were still happy as they were constantly second in the Western Conference and in the whole NBA with a record of 47-9, behind only the historical season that the Warriors are having.

Because of the Spurs' winning ways, Kawhi Leonard, together with new acquisition LaMarcus Aldridge, were named to the Western Conference All-Stars. It was Leonard's first trip to the All-Star game and he was a starter after the fans gave him a late push for the final starting slot. He scored 17 points in his first ever midseason classic, one that was held in Toronto, Canada. Shortly after the All-Star break, Kawhi Leonard was listed as questionable due to some tightness in his left calf. The reigning Defensive Player of the Year was rested longer after the break in order to have him at his best for the remainder of the season. Kawhi Leonard is currently averaging 20.2 points, 6.7 rebounds, and 1.8 steals while shooting 51% from the floor and an NBA-leading 48.2% from three-point territory. Even with Aldridge in the lineup, there was no question that Kawhi Leonard was the best player on the Spurs on both ends of the floor as he had evolved from being a defensive specialist into one of the most feared two-way players in the world.

Chapter 5: Kawhi Leonard's Personal Life

Kawhi's mother was Kim Robertson. His father was the late Mark Leonard. Kim and Mark divorced when their son was five years old. Mark owned and operated a car wash in Compton. He was the one who first exposed Kawhi to the game of basketball and instilled to him the basics of the sport such as the proper shooting form. Other than teaching his son basketball, Mark taught Kawhi the importance of hard work and perseverance in any aspect of life other than basketball. Under his supervision, Kawhi's school grades were constantly good as his father had always told him that studies should come first. Mark Leonard was murdered on January 18, 2008. He was closing up shop in his car wash when a group of men gunned him down in a possible robbery attempt.

Kawhi Leonard has close family ties to his mother's side of the family. Kim, Kawhi's mother, now resides with him in San Antonio. Kim does all the house work so Kawhi can focus on his basketball career. That was the least she could do as the mother of one of the fastest rising NBA stars. His grandmother, Wanda Robertson, was always close to her grandson, and she has said that Kawhi was always a Moreno Valley guy in that he always found a way to give back to the community. His uncle, Dennis Robertson, was his second father figure after his parents divorced. Dennis was the man that Kawhi looked up to after the death of Mark. Dennis also helped Kawhi in coping up with the death of Mark and with the rigors of growing up, especially when it came to money matters. With the help of Dennis, Kawhi has avoided being a spendthrift.

Unknown to the mainstream media, Kawhi Leonard has four sisters. All four of his sisters are older than he is and were from his mother Kim's previous relationship. He is also the cousin of Stevie Johnson, a professional football player playing in the National Football League under the San Diego Chargers.

Football indeed also runs in the blood as Kawhi used to play football in high school. Kawhi's girlfriend is Kishele Shipley, a San Diego native. The two met when Kawhi was still studying at San Diego State. She has since relocated to San Antonio after Leonard was drafted by the Spurs.

Chapter 6: Kawhi Leona.

and Future

Kawhi Leonard is such a unique basketbѯ

it's hard to compare or contrast him to aı. ⸜ıst and present NBA player. Standing at 6'7" and weighing 230 lbs., Leonard is a physical specimen of a man. With a wingspan that spans at almost 7'4" and with hands measured at nearly a foot long, Kawhi is a freak of nature. There have been a lot of players with Kawhi's combination of size and length. Such players are George Gervin, Kevin Garnett, Gerald Wallace, and Kevin Durant, among others. But somehow, Leonard is nothing like those players.

George Gervin was a pioneer in the NBA and scored a ton of points using his length and his patented finger roll layup. But he was not the defensive gem and rebounding demon that Kawhi Leonard is. Kevin Garnett was one of the most versatile players at his position because of his length, but his versatility and ooting range were not as deadly as Leonard's. He also could not move as nimbly as Kawhi does. Gerald Wallace was a player Leonard was compared to before his draft. Wallace was a good rebounder and a solid player on both ends of the court. But he did not have the shooting touch or the defensive tenacity that Leonard displays on the floor night in and night out. Lastly, Kevin Durant has the same amount of length and nimbleness that Leonard displays on the court. But Durant pours all of his energy into scoring while Leonard is a player that puts a hundred percent on both ends of the court.

With all that said, it is safe to assume that there has been nobody in the history of the NBA like Kawhi Leonard. Leonard came into the NBA as a defensive and rebounding savant. Gregg Popovich of the Spurs initially utilized Leonard's services solely and mainly on the defensive end. He has always been disciplined on defense and has a penchant for getting steals as he knows how to utilize his length at the passing lanes.

Because of his gifts on the defensive end, Kawhi Leonard has become one of the best, if not the best, perimeter players in the league. He consistently guards the opponents' best perimeter players, whether it be Carmelo Anthony, Kevin Durant, or Stephen Curry.

On defense, not a lot of players can stop LeBron James. James is a bull of a player with his size, strength, and athleticism. Other than that, LeBron also has a lot of skills on the offensive end to utilize against any defender. Put a capable but smaller player on him, and LeBron will bully him on the post. Put a big player on him, James will quickly blow past him to the basket. But put Kawhi Leonard on him and LeBron struggles. That's right. Kawhi has been one of the most active defenders on LeBron James as seen from their meeting in the NBA Finals twice.

LeBron usually struggles against Kawhi's defense. It's not that he could not make shots, but that he struggles to put even them up. Leonard is every bit of a physical freak that LeBron is, and he also contends with him athletically. Kawhi's length has also bothered James, and the four-time MVP finds it difficult to see a shot that he likes whenever Leonard is on him. In the 2014 Finals, only 17% of LeBron's touches turned into shots. In 35% of the Heat's possessions, LeBron could not even touch the ball. With Kawhi defending him, James has only attempted to drive on 13% of his possessions because Leonard could easily keep up with his quickness. Those numbers show how much of a gifted defender Kawhi Leonard is, and it's safe to say that he is indeed the LeBron James stopper.

As he gained experience, Kawhi Leonard became a terrific offensive player. He has a sweet shooting touch that extends all the way out to 25 feet away from the basket. He is deadly from outside the arc and has also displayed a good touch from midrange. Kawhi Leonard's offensive game also dwells inside the paint as he has also developed his game in the low post, particularly his turnaround jump shot. With his big hands, Kawhi Leonard dribbles and takes care of the ball well. And along with his long strides and with his superior athleticism, he can quickly attack the basket with ferocious dunks or tough layups.

As Kawhi Leonard evolved from being a defender to a great two-way player, he has become an NBA champion, a Finals MVP, an All-Star starter, and a Defensive Player of the Year while leading the San Antonio Spurs in both offense and defense. There is certainly no doubt that he is now the Spurs' best player as he has grown from being merely a project into the player that could usher in the future of the San Antonio organization, just as Tim Duncan ushered in a new Spurs era after David Robinson had gone past his prime years. The Spurs are already Kawhi's team and once the trio of Duncan, Parker, and Ginobili all decide to hang up their sneakers, the leadership reigns over the San Antonio franchise is all in the hands of Leonard.

It was also a play of fate for Kawhi and the San Antonio Spurs that he landed on the team he is playing right now. The Spurs wanted Kawhi as they traded a young and capable point guard for him to don a silver and black jersey. They had long wanted a player that could rebound and defend the wings much like what Bruce Bowen did for them in their championship runs in the 2000's. Kawhi did that and more for the Spurs as he was an even better upgrade of Bowen.

But on Kawhi's part, he was even more fortunate to have been drafted by San Antonio. The Spurs have a long history of finding gems in the draft. They drafted Manu Ginobili late in the second round back in 1999, and he became one of the most elusive sixth men the league has seen. They picked Tony Parker as the 28th overall draftee in 2001, and he became a multiple-time All-Star. Though the Spurs had a way of judging talent outside of the usual norms, the organization itself is also naturally good at finding players with great work ethic and they were even better at developing these players into All-Star caliber ballers. Kawhi Leonard was coming into the NBA with a lot of raw but unrealized talent on both offense and defense. It was indeed destiny that the Spurs wanted him in San Antonio as that organization was probably the only franchise in the NBA that could unlock all the hidden potential within Leonard.

As Kawhi Leonard's skills and talents as a player grew, so did his relationship with the Spurs' original Big Three of Tim Duncan, Tony Parker, and Manu Ginobili. Those three players are will no doubt be in the Hall of Fame soon and Kawhi was also fortunate enough to have learned a thing or two from them. Arguably the best power forward in the league and one of the most soft-spoken players, Tim Duncan has acted as a role model for Leonard. Duncan has always kept himself under the radar and has always been emotionless as Kawhi has always been but he was still an active leader on both ends of the court for the Spurs. Leonard, being similar to Duncan regarding how he brings himself up, is lucky to be under the wings of arguably one of the best players to have ever been in the NBA.

He also learned a couple of lessons from Parker and Ginobili as they have all been unheralded in their respective draft classes but then became All-Stars and NBA champions. A lot of Kawhi's work ethic is an offshoot from the two backcourt members of the Spurs' Big Three. While we always say that Kawhi Leonard was lucky to have landed with the San Antonio Spurs because of how the organization develops overlooked draftees into capable NBA professionals, he is even more fortunate that he was teammates with three consummate professional basketball players like Duncan, Parker, and Ginobili, who have contributed to the development and growth of one of the NBA's brightest young stars.

Acting as a bridge between the Big Three era and the Spurs' future, Kawhi Leonard has proven to the world that he has what it takes to be the next franchise superstar of the San Antonio Spurs organization. He came into the league when both Duncan and Ginobili were way past their prime years and when Parker was the best player in San Antonio. As he grew into his potential and his team, Kawhi Leonard has taken over the reins of the franchise. While Duncan and Ginobili are nearing their retirement years, only Parker will remain as the sole member of the original Big Three. But then again, Tony has seen a recent decline due to age. Nevertheless, he still has enough fuel in the tank left to help Leonard usher in a new era of Spurs basketball after the current period ends. When Kawhi finally becomes the sole franchise superstar of the team, a lot of his future success will be thanks to how he has grown under the wings of the Big Three much like how they grew and learned under the tutelage of David Robinson, Avery Johnson, and Bruce Bowen and many other long-retired Spurs legends.

As a Spur, Kawhi Leonard still has years to go before he could claim a spot on top of the franchise's best players. The San Antonio Spurs is are proud championship organization with a lot of historically great and legendary players like George Gervin, David Robinson, Tim Duncan, Manu Ginobili, and Tony Parker. While it's still too early to compare Kawhi to the careers of those players, if Kawhi Leonard stays with the Spurs for another decade and if he continues his terrific play as the best two-way player in the NBA, there is no doubt in anyone's mind that he can already be included in the conversation with the likes of Duncan, Robinson, and Gervin as the franchise's best player in history.

In the present-day NBA, Kawhi Leonard has shown his mettle as both a terrific two-way player and as one of the most famous ballers in the world. Leonard has been averaging about 20 points per game while also contributing his best on rebounding and defense. He leads the Spurs in scoring every night while also guarding the opponent's best players. With that in mind, it is arguable that Kawhi Leonard might perhaps be the best two-way wing player in the whole world. Popularity-wise, Kawhi Leonard has been voted as a starter in the 2016 All-Star game even while playing in the small market Spurs, and even as he barely shows any emotion or inclination to media attention. Leonard lets his game do the talking, and if he keeps the pace up for a lot more years, he will be remembered in the history of the NBA as a silent assassin who plays the game on both ends of the floor at the highest level possible. Kawhi is still young and is still far from his prime as an NBA player. Watch out, world. Kawhi Leonard is still growing and is coming just as swift and as silent as a sudden earthquake.

Final Word/About the Author

I was born and raised in Norwalk, Connecticut. Growing up, I could often be found spending many nights watching basketball, soccer, and football matches with my father in the family living room. I love sports and everything that sports can embody. I believe that sports are one of most genuine forms of competition, heart, and determination. I write my works to learn more about influential athletes in the hopes that from my writing, you the reader can walk away inspired to put in an equal if not greater amount of hard work and perseverance to pursue your goals. If you enjoyed *Kawhi Leonard: The Inspiring Story of One of Basketball's Best All-Around Players*, please leave a review! Also, you can read more of my works on *Colin Kaepernick, Aaron Rodgers, Peyton Manning, Tom Brady, Russell Wilson, Michael Jordan, LeBron James, Kyrie Irving, Klay Thompson, Stephen Curry, Kevin Durant, Russell Westbrook, Anthony Davis, Chris Paul, Blake Griffin, Kobe Bryant, Joakim*

Noah, Scottie Pippen, Carmelo Anthony, Kevin Love, Grant Hill, Tracy McGrady, Vince Carter, Patrick Ewing, Karl Malone, Tony Parker, Allen Iverson, Hakeem Olajuwon, Reggie Miller, Michael Carter-Williams, John Wall, James Harden, Tim Duncan, Steve Nash, Pau Gasol, Marc Gasol, Jimmy Butler, Dirk Nowitzki, Draymond Green and Pete Maravich in the Kindle Store. If you love basketball, check out my website at <u>claytongeoffreys.com</u> to join my exclusive list where I let you know about my latest books and give you lots of goodies.

Like what you read? Please leave a review!

I write because I love sharing the stories of influential people like Kawhi Leonard with fantastic readers like you. My readers inspire me to write more so please do not hesitate to let me know what you thought by leaving a review! If you love books on life, basketball, or productivity, check out my website at claytongeoffreys.com to join my exclusive list where I let you know about my latest books. Aside from being the first to hear about my latest releases, you can also download a free copy of *33 Life Lessons: Success Principles, Career Advice & Habits of Successful People*. See you there!

Clayton